KANSAS CITY
THEN & NOW

KANSAS CITY THEN & NOW

DARLENE ISAACSON

THUNDER BAY
P·R·E·S·S

San Diego, California

Thunder Bay Press
An imprint of the Advantage Publishers Group
5880 Oberlin Drive, San Diego, CA 92121-4794
www.thunderbaybooks.com

Produced by Salamander Books
151 Freston Road
London W10 6TH, United Kingdom
An imprint of Anova Books Ltd

© 2006 Salamander Books

ISBN-13: 978-1-59223-487-5
ISBN-10: 1-59223-487-9

Library of Congress Cataloging-in-Publication Data available on request.

1 2 3 4 5 11 10 09 08 07

Printed in China.

ACKNOWLEDGMENTS

I would like to thank the Kansas City Public Library Missouri Valley Room and Internet sites and its
Special Collections librarian, Sherrie Kline Smith; the Landmarks Division at City Hall of Kansas City
and Heather Gilbride; staffs of Immaculate Conception Catholic Church and Grace and Holy Trinity
Cathedral; Thomas Atkin, Barney White, and William Eddy; employees at SSA; and my husband, Max
Isaacson, for his encouragement and competent assistance. I would also like to credit the following sources
for providing information for this book: *Proud Heritage* by Robert S. Townsend, ed. (Kansas City Life
Insurance Company) and *A History of Kansas City, Missouri* by A. Theodore Brown and Lyle W. Dorsett.

PICTURE CREDITS

The publisher wishes to thank the following for kindly supplying the photographs that appear in this book:

"Then" photographs:
All "Then" photographs are courtesy of Missouri Valley Special Collections, Kansas City Public Library,
Kansas City, Missouri, except for the following:
Kansas City Historic Preservation/Landmarks Commission: p. 12, p. 14.
Kansas City City Hall Landmarks Division: p. 122.
Library of Congress, Prints and Photographs Division: p. 28 [LC-USZ62-125644], p. 42 [PAN US GEOG],
p. 120 [pan 6a07254], p. 128 [pan 6a07198], p. 140 [pan 6a07173].
Library of Congress, Prints and Photographs Division, Detroit Publishing Company Collection: p. 30 [LC-
D419-118], p. 52 [LC-D4-19226], p. 56 [LC-D4-19219], p. 106 [LC-D4-19222].

"Now" photographs:
All "Now" images were taken by Simon Clay (© Anova Image Library).

Anova Books is committed to respecting the intellectual property rights of others. We have therefore taken
all reasonable efforts to ensure that the reproduction of all content on these pages is done with the full
consent of copyright owners. If you are aware of any unintentional omissions, please contact the company
directly so that any necessary corrections may be made for future editions.

INTRODUCTION

"Everything's up to date in Kansas City" is one of the well-known lines from Rodgers and Hammerstein's 1943 musical *Oklahoma!* The words are still as relevant today, as Kansas City experiences its biggest building boom since the turn of the twentieth century. Some of the city's newest developments include the oval-shaped H&R Block International Headquarters, the 18,500-seat arena Sprint Center, and the expanded Bartle Hall Convention Center, as well as many new lofts, studios, and condominiums. Historic hotels have been renovated to their former elegance, helping to bring more visitors to Kansas City's attractions: the Nelson-Atkins Museum of Art, the American Jazz Museum, its football and baseball franchises, and the popular theme park Worlds of Fun, among others.

The territories of Kansas and Western Missouri were part of the Louisiana Purchase of 1803. The earliest inhabitants were the Kansa, Osage, and Wyandotte Indians, as well as a small community of Creole French traders from St. Louis. The first white settler in Jackson County, Missouri, was Daniel Morgan Boone (1769–1839), one of the pioneers from Kentucky and son of the famous frontiersman Daniel Boone. After discovering what would later become Kansas City, the younger Boone guided others to the new frontier. In 1821, Francois Chouteau, known as the "King of the Fur Trade," and his wife Bernice came to the confluence of the Kaw and Missouri rivers to set up their trading post and first home on the banks of the barren bluffs.

Many early settlers' occupations were tied to the country's expansion. The area truly was a gateway to the West—as the aptly named town of Westport (established in 1833) testified. Settlers would disembark the steamboat in Independence and outfit their wagons before setting out on the Santa Fe Trail. This all changed when Westport trader John McCoy began using a rock ledge, near what is today First and Grand, to unload goods from the steamboat. The ledge was known as the Westport Landing in the Town of Kansas. McCoy's discovery saved people an entire day of travel because he shipped goods to Westport Landing and then hauled them to the Westport Trading Post. Derived from the name of its first inhabitants, the Town of Kansas was incorporated by the state in 1853, and then shortened its name to Kansas City in 1889.

In the 1800s, several settlements, including Leavenworth and St. Joseph, were competing for the first railroad bridge to cross the Missouri River—an instrumental move in developing the West. Missouri senator Thomas Hart Benton chose Kansas City. Hannibal Bridge, which crossed the Missouri River at Broadway Avenue, was constructed in 1869 and led to growth in the stockyards and the grain industry. Cattle and swine were shipped in by rail after grazing south and west of Kansas City, where they were processed before being sent to St. Louis and Chicago. The meatpacking industry was born in the West Bottoms, close to the railroad lines. The pervading smell in the area prompted the nickname "Cow Town"—more favorably referred to as "the smell of money" by those who lived there. The term was accurate in the 1800s when fortunes were made as the cattlemen sold their livestock and profits soared in banking, restaurants, lodging, and the retail and entertainment industries.

Early Kansas City was not a place for the timid. Fortunes were made on paper and lost just as quickly. In addition to the purveyors of goods to the Santa Fe Trail, there were entrepreneurs selling everything from clothing to food, as well as the materials necessary for the buildings that were springing up all around. The dirt streets soon became wooden and were later paved with bricks, while shops were given awnings to protect their customers from sun and rain.

The years preceding the Civil War were turbulent ones. Many settlers came from the Northern states, but some, like John Wornall, came from the South. Wornall, who arrived from Kentucky with his four slaves in 1843, went on to become one of Kansas City's most successful farmers. When the war began there was no clear-cut loyalty to either side. Business leaders in Kansas City supported the Union cause; Fort Union was located at the site of the Kersey Coates Hotel. The Pacific Hotel was a Union headquarters, where the famous edicts were written to clear the border areas of civilians before of the Battle of Westport. The war caused extreme hardship for most Missouri farmers near Kansas City when they were forced from their farms, leaving unharvested crops in the field.

City expansion continued after the Civil War ended as the city grew with an influx of immigrants. From Quality Hill, residents moved to the east, where they found new apartments along tree-lined avenues with fountains. Streetcars ran all the way to the new Swope Park and Westport, which had become a less-dominant force and was officially annexed into Kansas City in 1899. The West Bottoms experienced major floods, disrupting railroad travel at Union Depot and forcing the post office and train depot to relocate to Nineteenth and Main. By the turn of the twentieth century, many businessmen were concerned about the growing hodgepodge of downtown buildings and industry. Influential men organized a "City Beautiful" campaign and addressed their concerns about urban development by hiring landscaper George Kessler and city planner Adrian Van Brunt to ensure green spaces. By the 1920s, wealthy merchants had built large estates as far south as Forty-fifth and Oak and J. C. Nichols developed the elegant Country Club Plaza—the world's first shopping center designed to accommodate the automobile.

Kansas City suffered during the Great Depression, but major building projects, including City Hall, Jackson County Courthouse, and the Municipal Auditorium offered much-needed work. Following World War II, expansion to the suburbs accelerated while African Americans moved into the residential areas south and west of Fortieth and Troost. The late 1950s marked the end of segregation in schools, transportation, and recreation and by the 1970s housing throughout the city became available to all.

The 1970s saw a slowdown in the development of downtown and its business centers. Hotels closed and it seemed that new businesses were choosing suburban locations. These conditions lasted until the 1990s, when companies started to buy and renovate old buildings, like the New York Life Building and the Muehlebach Hotel, and transform historic garment district warehouses into modern living spaces.

Kansas City today exemplifies its "City Beautiful" movement—it is believed to have more boulevards than Paris and more fountains than any other city in the world beside Rome. Known as the "Heart of America," Kansas City is also thoroughly modern. With its cutting-edge medical research centers, state-of-the-art buildings, and its many new loft apartments, everything really is up to date in Kansas City.

These first buildings of the Country Club Plaza, at the junction of Forty-seventh and Main streets, were constructed along Mill Creek by J. C. Nichols Company in 1922. This 1930 photograph shows the Spanish-style Mill Creek Building, America's first planned shopping center, for which fountains and statuary were imported from all over the world. Nichols was a planner of unequaled stature and used this shopping center to develop residential areas to the south, aimed at middle- and upper-income families. His ideas for sound construction and style were appealing and combined with his knowledge of the terrain and his cooperation with landscape architect George Kessler, Nichols created a pleasant, livable community.

The Country Club Plaza today is even more vibrant and colorful than when it opened. The beautiful Horse Fountain was created by Parisian sculptor Henri Greber in 1910 and is dedicated to the memory of the plaza's founder. Originally located in the gardens of the Clarence H. Mackay Estate in Roslyn, New York, the fountain was brought to Kansas City in 1952 and restored and dedicated in 1960. The quality of the shops leasing space here is still very high and the center is kept up exceptionally well. Always customer-friendly, the number

and caliber of restaurants adds to the ambience of the area. The Country Club Plaza is world-renowned for its miles of Christmas lights that outline the buildings. People gather here every year for the much-photographed Plaza Lighting Ceremony on Thanksgiving night. The tradition of the lights began in 1929 when a maintenance worker hung a single strand of Christmas lights over a door frame.

The site of Saint Luke's Hospital at 4401 Wornall was originally the location of the first house built in Westport. John Calvin McCoy, the house's owner and the town's founder, operated a general store, trading with the Indians and outfitting the immigrants' wagon trains as they headed west. Like the settlers, the hospital picked up and moved as well: in 1923, Saint Luke's Hospital left its first location at Tenth and Campbell streets, where it had a fifty-bed facility, for a new six-story, 150-bed facility on Wornall Road. This photograph, taken in 1950, shows the hospital after it expanded to serve the surrounding community.

Today, Saint Luke's is a 629-bed hospital covering eight square blocks, and includes a dozen facilities employing nearly five hundred physicians in all areas of medical expertise. They are dedicated to the highest levels of patient care, research, and education. The Saint Luke's health-care system includes a nursing school in the Wornall complex and other hospitals in the metropolitan area. In 2005 it initiated a $200-million renovation, which will construct a new Mid-America Heart Institute, the Kauffman Women's Heart Center, and the Center for Women and Infants.

Built in 1927 in the Spanish Renaissance Revival style by George Miller and Guy McCandless, the Locarno (at left in this 1938 image) and Villa Serena (center) apartments are located at 300 and 325 Ward Parkway. The footbridge crossing Brush Creek gave residents easy access to the south edge of the Country Club Plaza. Barney Goodman, a Jewish immigrant, came to Kansas City to own and operate the Locarno and Villa Serena as well as several other apartments and hotels, including the Bellerive, Carlisle, Newbern, and Sophian Plaza.

In 1975, the Pistilli family purchased the Villa Serena and turned it into the Raphael Hotel. The 123-room hotel has been ranked among the best hotels in the world and is listed on the National Register of Historic Places. After thirty years, the Pistilli family sold the hotel to Lighthouse Properties of Salina, Kansas. The Locarno is still operating as an apartment building and is joined on the block by the St. Regis, Hemingway, and Casa Loma apartments. A new footbridge now connects the buildings with the plaza. In keeping with the plaza's art tradition, a statue of Winston Churchill and his wife Winnie stands across the street from the Raphael Hotel.

Reverend Nathan Scarritt came to Kansas City from Virginia in 1852 to pastor Methodist churches. Before long, the thirty-one-year-old Scarritt started Westport High School, where he also taught. This home at 4038 Central was built in 1852 by Dr. J. O. Boggs and was occupied by Scarritt and his wife, Martha Matilda Chick, the daughter of William and Ann Chick, who purchased the Westport general store from John McCoy. After buying land on the bluffs overlooking the East Bottoms in 1862, Scarritt moved from the Westport area and built a log cabin to ensure the safety of his family as the country moved toward civil war. Land investments in the downtown area made Scarritt one of the richest men in Kansas City by 1880. This 1940s surveyor's office photograph includes a handheld board, which was used to identify properties and determine their taxes.

Scarritt's home is now a museum and tribute to the family man who was an early preacher, educator, and Indian agent. Scarritt's office building is still in use at 819 Walnut. His move to the northeastern part of the city led to the development of the area called Scarritt's Point, where his original log cabin was built. He later built his permanent home there, as well as homes for his children. These large, stately homes can be identified today by their use of limestone materials native to the area. His Scarritt's Point home is still occupied by family members today.

The house at 3616 Belleview was built in 1903 for Walter E. Kirkpatrick, treasurer of the Kansas City Electric Company. This impressive home, seen here in the 1940s, was designed by architect George Matthews Engeles. The large wooded lot with its stone edging and matching stone foundation made the home blend perfectly with nature. It was purchased in 1939 by artist Thomas Hart Benton and was used as his home and studio for over thirty-five years. After studying at the Art Institute of Chicago and in Paris, Benton came to Kansas City to be an instructor at the Kansas City Art Institute. Benton's father was a congressman from Missouri and his grand-uncle was Missouri's first senator, Thomas Hart "Old Bullion" Benton.

The home is now a museum dedicated to Thomas Hart Benton and his murals, which depict the laborers who toiled in America in the 1930s. His murals can be seen in the Missouri State Capitol in Jefferson City and at the Truman Library in Independence. Benton's masterpiece, *Persephone* (circa 1938), is held at Nelson-Atkins Museum of Art in Kansas City. His home and studio are kept much as they were when he died, paintbrush in hand, on January 19, 1975. The museum is operated as a State Historic Site and is open to the public for tours.

Kansas City Life Insurance was established in 1895, marketing life insurance, annuities, and group insurance. Pictured here in 1945 is the Corinthian-style office built in 1925 on Armour and Broadway by the Collins Construction Company. At the same time, Collins Construction was building two other Kansas City landmarks—the Nelson-Atkins Museum of Art and the First National Bank. The limestone used in all three buildings came from the same Indiana quarry. The lionesses (see opposite) were modeled after two lions at the Swope Park Zoo. Eleven feet long and five feet high, the statues reflect the theme of the company, "She Protects Her Own." Kansas City sculptor Jorgen Dreyer, a native of Norway, carved the beautiful lionesses. Dreyer's first employer was the Fine Arts Institute (later called the Art Institute).

In 1984, when more office space was needed for the insurance company, the builders contacted the same quarry in Indiana. Limestone from that exact area was available to provide a perfect match for the new offices. Always a believer in supporting arts in the workplace, Kansas City Life Insurance commissioned seventy-five watercolors by artist Frederick James on the company's seventy-fifth anniversary. Dreyer's lionesses still guard the entrance to the building; on the company's hundredth anniversary the front plaza was spruced up with a Kugel—a sphere floating on water, made by Midwest Titan Inc. The one-ton red granite ball is supported at the base only by water jets, and can be moved in any direction with just the touch of a fingertip. Today's staff includes six hundred associates in the home office.

The Scout was executed by Cyrus E. Dallin of Boston for exhibition at the Panama-Pacific Exposition in San Francisco in 1915. As the statue was transported back to the East Coast, it was displayed in Penn Valley Park. The sixteen-foot bronze Indian on horseback was so appealing to the people of Kansas City that they raised $15,000 in small donations so that it could become a permanent fixture in Penn Valley Park. Many of the donations were said to have come from schoolchildren. The four tallest buildings visible in this 1933 photograph are, from the left, the Power and Light Building, the Fidelity Bank and Trust Building, the Jackson County Courthouse, and City Hall of Kansas City.

The Scout still presides over Penn Valley Park. Access to the statue is only available via the BMA tower. Originally the Business Men's Association, this building has since been converted into modern loft apartments. Visitors to Penn Valley Park are treated to a spectacular view of downtown Kansas City and the confluence of the Missouri and Kaw rivers. Over the years,

The Scout has been vandalized; arrows have been taken from his quiver, the feather from his head. Happily, his recently cleaned and repaired condition make him one of the most beautiful sights in the city and worth many times over his initial cost.

Howard Vanderslice commissioned this statue in honor of his mother, Sara Jane Vanderslice, who made the journey from Kentucky to Kansas City with her husband, Major Daniel Vanderslice, an Indian agent for the United States government. The sculptor chosen was Alexander Phimister Proctor and the statue was given to the people of Kansas City on November 11, 1927. A pink granite pedestal has the biblical inscription, "Whither thou goest, I will go, whither thou lodgest, I will lodge. Thy people shall be my people, and thy God, my God." The *Pioneer Mother* faces the beginnings of the Santa Fe Trail, which traversed Penn Valley Park just a few feet from her statue. In the background of this 1927 photograph is the Liberty Memorial.

A visit to Penn Valley Park and the nearby Liberty Memorial shows the *Pioneer Mother* as powerful and meaningful today as it was at its dedication in 1927. Today the site surrounding the statue is enhanced and softened by the plantings around the base of the pedestal, but it is in such good condition that it is hard to believe it has withstood the elements of Kansas City weather for almost eighty years. When Howard Vanderslice donated the statue, which cost him $100,000, it was a gift for many generations of Kansas Citians. The Liberty Memorial was recently renovated and offers breathtaking views of downtown.

This photograph from 1945 shows the area at Main Street and Pershing Road from the east side of Main. The steep bluff just ten blocks from the heart of the city had long been an overgrown wasteland. Toward the end of the nineteenth century, a few houses were built on top of the bluff but erosion and access for streets, services, and utilities had become such a problem that it was largely deserted. For years, the name Signboard Hill had been assigned to this area because that seemed to be its only practical use.

In 1968, Hallmark Cards Inc.'s founder, Joyce C. Hall, implemented his vision of an entertainment center that would incorporate both permanent residents and hotels sharing the district with commercial ventures. The international headquarters of Hallmark is located within the eighty-five-acre Crown Center complex. Hotels in the center include the 729-room Westin Crown Center and the 731-room Hyatt Regency Crown Center. Broadway-type stage shows, a multiscreen movie complex, and a wide variety of restaurants have made this center a destination for the traveler as well as area residents. This view shows the Westin Crown Center Hotel, San Francisco Towers, and the San Francisco Office Building in the foreground, with the Hyatt Regency in the background. In the left lower corner is the Link, a crosswalk for pedestrians that connects the Crown Center Hotel, Union Station, and the Hyatt Regency Hotel.

The Sweeney Auto School at 215 West Pershing can be seen at the left of this 1926 photograph. The structure was designed by architects Arthur S. Keene and Leslie B. Simpson and had 550 rooms. The original plans had a swimming pool in the basement so that the building could be used as a hotel if the school failed. The school was built and owned by Emory J. Sweeney in the early 1900s, when automobiles had just started to become more common. The school trained over five thousand men during World War I. In 1918, a flu epidemic swept through more than three thousand men enrolled at the automobile school. Fifteen mechanics died during the reverse-quarantine designed to protect the Army men from civilians. After the school failed financially in 1929, the Business Men's Assurance Company bought and renovated the building for its use until 1962, when they moved to Thirty-first and Southwest Trafficway.

The large expanse of concrete at the intersection of Pershing and Main that was once shared by cars, streetcars, horses, and carriages has been reshaped to handle the flow of modern-day traffic. The Link that connects both Union Station (visible to the right) and the Hyatt Regency complex cuts Pershing Road just east of Main Street. Across Pershing on the west side, a beautiful fountain serves as a median to divide the traffic into two east-west lanes. Just under the Link is Washington Park, complete with a bronze equestrian statue of George Washington. The monument was designed by Henry Shrady and has graced the park since 1925. Today the Sweeney building's upper floors are occupied but the ground level is available for restaurant leasing.

Before the Federal Post Office at 315 West Pershing was built, residents called the area Cox's Pasture or the OK Creek. Because of drainage issues and extensive sewer problems, it was under construction from 1912 until 1922, at a cost of $4 million. When the post office was dedicated in 1933, hundreds of people filled the frontage lined with flags and patriotic decorations. Shown here in 1945, the structure was made of cement from Thomas Pendergast's company and ornamental carvings were made at the KC Cut Stone Company. This midtown location gave ample room for the expansion of services that were needed as Kansas City's population expanded. The post office had originally been part of the Federal Building at Ninth and Walnut and also had operations in the West Bottoms, which were often flooded.

After seventy years of use, the Federal Post Office building was deemed too small and a new lease was negotiated with the Internal Revenue Service. Senator Kit Bond was instrumental in obtaining the $370 million slated for the project with an extensive expansion to the south and west. This photograph shows renovation work in progress on the main building and a walkway connecting the new addition. The renovated building will be used by more than four thousand full-time employees and two thousand seasonal employees. Postal operations in the area will shift over to Union Station's space across Pershing Road and give Union Station much-needed revenue.

After the signing of the Treaty of Versailles in 1919, there were celebrations and fund-raisers for war memorials throughout the United States. Over $2 million was raised in Kansas City and at the conclusion of a national competition, H. Van Buren Magonigle's Liberty Memorial design was chosen. After the tower and museum (out of frame, to the left of this picture) were completed in 1921, a grand dedication ceremony was held. As this photograph taken in front of Union Station shows, thousands of people were in attendance, with a crowd of two hundred thousand filling Pershing Road alone. Vice President Calvin Coolidge, Allied war leaders—Lieutenant General Baron Jacques of Belgium, General Armando Diaz of Italy, Marshall Ferdinand Foch of France, General John J. Pershing of the United States, Admiral Lord Earl Beatty of Great Britain—and many color guard units made the day one Kansas City has long remembered.

In 1998, Kansas City voted to impose a one-half cent sales tax for the next eighteen years to both restore the Liberty Memorial and establish an endowment fund to maintain the facility. The renovation began in the spring of 2000 and was completed in time for Memorial Day, 2002. The courtyards and stonework of the museum building were redesigned, cleaned, and replaced. Expansion of exhibition space has given the museum more educational display areas and its facilities have been improved in compliance with the Americans with Disabilities Act without devaluing the building's architectural integrity. Bronze busts of the five Allied leaders who attended the original site dedication are displayed on the memorial's wall. The Sweeney Building is shown to the left of this photograph.

After Union Depot flooded in 1903, city leaders agreed that a new station was needed. The second station, accessible to downtown yet spacious enough to accommodate the railroads and people, was designed by Jarvis Hunt. Parades and a twenty-one-gun salute marked the grand opening on October 31, 1914. Union Station was the first building in the area to open, followed by the World War I Memorial and the federal post office. As this 1920s photograph shows, the enormous structure could accommodate over ten thousand people with its 352-foot-long waiting room, while covered walkways protected passengers as they arrived and departed by train. The station's most notorious event occurred during a transfer of gangster Frank Nash as he was being escorted to Leavenworth Prison. His cronies shot and killed four officers—and Nash himself—in a bungled attempt to help him escape.

Union Station was abandoned in 1983 because of leaking roofs, reduced railroad traffic, and general neglect. But in 1994, a bistate tax gave Union Station a new lease on life and it reopened in 1999 with nearly as much hoopla as its first opening as 1914. Now the fountains on Pershing Road provide an elegant welcome as visitors enter through the heavy wooden doors to see the station's completely restored interior. Marble floors and beautiful ceilings and windows have turned the station into a civic center that features fund-raising events, movie theaters, restaurants, and Science City and its planetarium. The imposing clock, a popular meeting spot, has been painstakingly restored, and artworks by Thomas Hart Benton Gude (grandson of artist Thomas Hart Benton) are on display. The contemporary office building at the far right in this photograph is called #2 Pershing Square.

The president of the Coca-Cola Company chose Kansas City as the site of his new plant in 1910 when he traversed the Midwest to find the right combination of labor and capital. He found the the perfect location just three blocks from Union Station, at Twenty-first and Grand Avenue. The pie-shaped building, pictured here in the 1920s, was designed by Arthur Tufts of Baltimore and built in 1915 by the Swenson Construction Company for just over a million dollars. The curved side of the building faces the railroad tracks. Western Auto Supply moved into the building in 1928.

After Western Auto purchased the building in 1951, they added their distinctive sign to the roof. However, the building was sold in 1998 to Advance Auto Parts, the new owners threatened to remove the Western Auto sign. There was such an outcry from the community over this possible action that the owners relented and the sign was restored with a special lighting ceremony held on April 10, 2003. The familiar fifty-eight-foot sign is visible from all over the city and has almost three thousand light bulbs and tubes of white neon. The building's conversion into lofts was completed in 2004 and an aggressive marketing plan sold all ninety-three units by the spring of 2006. In order to complete the sales, an auction was held for the last units.

This photograph of the Reid-Ward Motor Company, located at 2500 McGee Trafficway, was taken in 1928, at the peak of new automobile sales in Kansas City. The company's primary sales were generated by the Packard automobile. William David Packard and his brother James Ward Packard established the Packard Electric Company in 1890 in Warren, Ohio. They built the first Packard automobile in 1899 after forming the Ohio Automobile Company.

In 1911, their electric company was so profitable they were able to help light their city's streets for the first time in the United States. The Ohio Automobile Company (later called the Packard Motor Car Company) manufactured the Packard until 1932, when they became a division of General Motors. The Packard, which was known for its superior style and quality, was produced until 1958.

The Reid-Ward building was demolished in 1968 to make way for the Crown Center complex. On the same site today stands one division of the National Headquarters and Manufacturing Center for Hallmark Cards, Inc. The internationally known company has a market share of almost half of greeting card sales in the United States and they employ more than twenty-five thousand people worldwide. The founder of Hallmark was Joyce Hall, whose career began as a traveling salesman selling postcards. His first company was founded in 1915 and was eventually named Hallmark in 1928, after a goldsmith's symbol in London. In 1951, Hall began to sponsor television programs, which evolved into the award-winning *Hallmark Hall of Fame*. Today the chairman of the private Hallmark Company is Donald J. Hall Sr. and the president and CEO is Donald J. Hall Jr. The Hallmark Photographic Collection has been donated to the Nelson-Atkins Art Museum and will be on display in 2007.

The founding members of Children's Mercy Hospital were sisters Dr. Alice Berry Graham, a dentist, and Dr. Katherine Berry Richardson, a physician. The Mercy Hospital was founded shortly after a man from the local stockyards brought an abandoned five-year-old girl to the women. The compassion shown to this first patient has had an impact on Kansas City ever since. After opening the small hospital at Fifteenth and Cleveland, a blackboard was placed outside the clinic outlining the needs for the day. The hospital expanded its services and moved into another site at Independence Boulevard and Seventeenth Street in 1916. The sisters' vision remained to provide the best mental and physical care to any child, regardless of financial circumstances. This 1940s photograph shows the Twenty-fourth and Gillham Road site.

The Children's Mercy Hospital today represents the most modern and updated treatment facility for children. Continuous additions to the original building have supported more than forty pediatric specialties that serve the needs of a 150-county region in western Missouri and eastern Kansas. The hospital is recognized for its expertise in cardiac surgery, transplantation, nephrology, and neonatology. Its research programs specialize in clinical pharmacology, genetics, and neonatology. This 241-bed hospital has 40 percent of its inpatient rooms devoted to critical care. The hospital also provides services through a home health program available to many outpatients who are not covered by medical insurance. Celebrities often visit and contribute to fund-raising events, including golfer Tom Watson, a Kansas City native who has sponsored several charitable golf tournaments.

The Truman house at 219 North Delaware in Independence, eight miles east of Kansas City, was built in 1867 by the owner of a milling company, General Porterfield Gates. The style of the home, shown here in the 1940s, is referred to as Missouri River Gothic. Gates's daughter Madge resided in the house with her daughter Bess and her husband David W. Wallace, who died in 1908. After Harry Truman married Bess Wallace in 1919, they moved into the Delaware Street house. The three shared the home until Madge's death in 1952. Truman's early career as a banker began in Kansas City after he left his rural home near Grandview to supplement his parents' meager income. He worked at the National Bank of Commerce and later Union National Bank until he joined the army and served in World War I. Truman's brief career in the haberdashery business was over by 1922. That same year, he began his political career in the Democratic Party when he was elected as a judge in Jackson County.

During his fifty-three years living in Independence, Truman saw many changes. When he became president in 1945, this house was known as the "Independence White House," and though Harry died some twenty years after he was president, he was often seen in the neighborhood on brisk morning walks, a sprightly figure with a hat and cane in later years. The house has remained much the same through the years with its marble fireplaces, high ceilings, large living room, and a dining-room table that can seat thirty guests. The Truman residence is now open to the public and is maintained by the National Park Service.

Robert A. Long was a lumber executive who headed a vast chain of lumberyards, extending all the way from Kansas City to the logging city of Longview, Oregon, which he built with planning help from J. C. Nichols and George Kessler in 1918. When Long was planning his dream home, he investigated different locations in Hyde Park and Janssen Place. His love of the rugged terrain of North Terrace Park gave Long the inspiration to buy an entire block on Gladstone Boulevard. In 1909, he began construction of Corinthian Hall, a mansion designed by Henry Hoit in Beaux Arts style with an elaborate French interior. Pictured here in 1915, the seventy-room home included a large carriage house and stable. Long lived here with his wife Ella and his two daughters, Loula and Sallie.

After Long's death in 1934, his daughters donated his magnificent home at 3218 Gladstone Boulevard to the Kansas City Museum Association. In 1939, just one year after their donation, the Kansas City Museum of History and Science opened. By 1976, only the great hall had been restored to its original decor. Now that Union Station has been opened for science exhibits, it is anticipated that new restoration will return Corinthian Hall to its former French decor. In the carriage house, ornate carriages belonging to Loula Long Combs will be displayed along with many trophies, ribbons, and show harnesses from her years of showing and training Hackney horses. Union Station–Kansas City, Inc. is operator of the Kansas City Museum, which is open for visitors every day but Monday.

COLONNADE

W. H. Dunn, Kansas City's park superintendent, recommended paving the roadway at North Terrace Park, near Scarritt Point, in 1907. However, halfway through construction, he determined it was not a suitable place for "new automobiles." The Colonnade was built here in June 1908 by contractors J. B. Neevel and Son. From this point, visitors could view Cliff Drive, Missouri River Valley, the East Bottoms, and Clay County in the distance. The memorial boulder on the east side of the intersection (not visible in this 1910 photograph) is a tribute to Thomas Hart "Old Bullion" Benton, the first senator from Missouri in the United States Senate. Legislation he supported played a key role in opening the West, with funds coming to Missouri to build railroads, purchase land, and open the Oregon and Santa Fe trails.

Though the view is somewhat obscured by the large trees overlooking the roadway and valley below, the Colonnade is still a stately structure. The columns are in good condition after nearly one hundred years of use. An addition to the center of the main section was dedicated in May of 1965 to honor president John F. Kennedy. Post 151 of the American Legion, Department of Missouri, erected an eternal flame monument to remind passersby of Kennedy's service and sacrifice to his country.

This 1900 photograph shows men and women enjoying a day at Electric Park, eating and drinking near the main entrance. German bands often played by the tables, making it seem like a German beer garden. Electric Park capitalized on the invention of the light bulb, which helped to extend its evening hours and boost attendance. Visitors could look out and see all the lights in the valley below, called East Bottoms. The park was owned by the Joseph H. Heim Brewery and in the middle of this photograph, behind the flagpole, the large brick brewery is visible. The beer was piped directly to the beer garden in the foreground. There was easy access to the park by the Fifth Street car line, also owned by the brewery. During the summer, water features, boating and bathing facilities, and even a vaudeville theater made this a delightful place for a family outing. The facility closed its Montgall and Rochester location in 1908 and reopened at Forty-seventh and Paseo—only to be destroyed by fire in 1928.

These days the park is a quiet area during weekday daylight hours. Now you can drive north of Independence on Chestnut Avenue Trafficway, cutting right through the heart of the park. Still visible in the photograph is the old Heim Brewery building, now used for a wholesale flower warehouse. Just one block south of where the main entrance was at Montgall and Rochester is an old fire station made with bricks from the same era and which still bears the name Heim. The strains of music and laughter can still be heard on weekends and nights from Knucklehead's tavern, which has its own outdoor music area.

Built in 1910, the Masonic Temple was the headquarters of the Masons, one of the social and fraternal clubs so important in early Kansas City. With so many new people arriving in the city between the 1890s and 1920s, these clubs provided a crucial role in people's social lives. Note the color guards in the lower portion of this 1910 photograph and the dignitaries on the balcony on the right, who are assembled after a parade that would have taken them several blocks into the downtown area. The elaborate hats of the Masons indicate their importance and status in the organization.

The building at Ninth and Harrison now stands vacant, with barred windows, a crumbling foundation, and a deserted parking lot. From its early grandeur as an upscale meeting hall and place for social functions, it now faces almost certain destruction. The decline of many fraternal organizations and the movement of affluent city dwellers toward the expanding suburbs combined to make this downtown building a less-popular meeting place. The area, referred to as East Village, has been slated for demolition in the next phase of rebuilding downtown Kansas City.

The area along Twelfth and Holmes lay between downtown and the Paseo— a residential area that sprung up as the city expanded east. This expansion was partly due to the growing stockyards, whose unpleasant fumes forced West Bottoms residents to move east. The Paseo had fountains, arbors, and apartment homes along the avenue. After the depression of the 1930s, Twelfth and Holmes developed an increasing number of liquor stores and seedy hotels.

The Marquette Hotel, seen in the foreground of this 1945 picture, boasted pool, snooker, and "Liquors—by drink or package." However, one bright spot in the area (not shown in this picture) was Saint Mary's Episcopal Church. When the red brick building was built in 1888, it featured beautiful stained-glass windows, a marble altar designed by Tiffany, and Kansas City's first reed organ.

Saint Mary's Church is now dwarfed by Interstate 70 and the nineteen-story Federal Office Building. The area was cleared of many run-down shops in 1965, when construction began on the Federal Building site at Twelfth and Holmes. A large plaza on the northwest corner of the building and a statue in memory of the victims of the 1995 Oklahoma City bombing are two of the features that greet visitors to its the main entrance. Included in the building are a cafeteria, post office, gift shop, credit union, heath care unit, barbershop, exercise room, nursery, and playground. It is estimated that 20 percent of Kansas City's employees work for government agencies.

Kansas City's first city hall was near the historic city market area but it moved to this location at 414 East Twelfth in 1937. It took twenty-two months to complete this thirty-story Beaux Arts skyscraper. Backed by Kansas City's Democratic machine, the decision to build a new city hall was part of a ten-year bond program to prove that the depression was over. As part of the same bond program, the Jackson County Courthouse was built in 1934. Kansas City's city hall, seen here in 1938, is a 1930s engineering masterpiece. Its steel frame is encased in 20,000 cubic feet of concrete, 7,800 tons of stone, and 6,800 tons of steel. It has been calculated that the building grows almost 3.25 inches taller on hot summer days, and to allow for this expansion, an elastic compound was used instead of cement mortar on one row of stone on each floor.

The original building used such high-quality marble, paneling, and light fixtures that little interior refurbishing has been necessary. However, employees were thankful when the air-conditioning system that formerly cooled only the mayor's office was extended to the rest of the building. Since 1940, the council-manager form of government has been reinstated, and today the city hall houses almost fifteen hundred city employees. The observation deck on the building's thirtieth floor offers excellent views of Kansas City's latest developments, including the Sprint Center arena, the Power & Light district, and the H&R Block International Headquarters building. The city hall is located in the government district, which is centered around Ilus Davis Park and includes the Jackson County Courthouse and the Bolling Federal Office building.

Kansas City's library system was instituted in 1873. The first books of the new library were a set of American Encyclopedias purchased with the $100 that the library founders had raised. Patrons of the library could use its facilities for $2.00 a year, or they could purchase a lifetime membership for $10.00. Carrie Westlake Whitney was Kansas City's first librarian, with a salary of $30 per month. She held this position for over thirty years until her retirement in 1911. The city opened the first building at Eighth and Oak in 1889; eight years later the library moved to the beautiful building seen in this circa 1903 photograph, at Ninth and Locust. More than twenty thousand people visited this new structure the week it opened.

The building ceased to be used as a library when a new facility opened in 1961. Today the Victorian building at Ninth and Locust is dwarfed by the Charles Evans Whittaker Federal Courthouse, just west of the library (beyond the left edge of this picture). Under the eaves of the library building, the names of famous authors of classic literature are carved into the building's stone. The doors hint at the beautiful oak wood interior used in the original construction. The main occupant today is the Ozark Life Insurance Company. Kansas City's current library is located in the First National Bank building at Tenth and Baltimore.

This 1940s photograph shows the Planters Seed Company in River Market, opened in 1924 by German immigrant Henry Werthheim. Farmers would drop off their produce at the nearby market and then collect their seed supplies from Werthheim. The proximity of the building to the nearby market has always benefited the business.

Planters Seed Company has retained its name, its original redbrick facade, and its antique counters, but today's inventory includes fresh bulk spices, condiments, and gourmet coffees. The latest expansion of the business to include outdoor furniture and patio art has taken space to the south of the original building. Its reputation for excellent customer service has kept this locally owned store in business for more than eighty years.

The city market near Fourth and Walnut has always been a bustling place. When Kansas City built its first city hall—seen in the background of this 1906 picture—it was only natural that people came to carry out their business and then visit the nearby market stalls. The Gillis family donated the market area to Kansas City in 1840 for "public use forever" and in 1858 the first market buildings were built. Farmers brought their wagons, pulled them into the market square, and began selling to local housewives. The streetcar lines from outer areas gave access to the wares of the producers, eliminating any middleman fees and ensuring quick farm-to-table time. Awnings were added to shade the booths' produce—and their customers—on hot summer days. Stalls sold freshly killed meat, including deer and rabbit, alongside seasonal fruit and vegetables.

Through the years, the market has remained a colorful place to visit during the months of harvest. An Italian specialty shop and wine shop have joined the fresh produce vendors and the market has expanded to the west and south to form a square. In the center, covered spaces are leased weekly to local farmers, who sell their produce during the harvest season that begins in mid-May and ends in late fall. A wide variety of restaurants offer many choices of food if shoppers get hungry.

This photograph from 1868 shows Market Square from Third and Walnut, with a hot-air balloon readying for takeoff as part of the Fourth of July celebrations. The city's earliest known balloon designer was Mrs. William Ragan, wife of the first professional photographer in Kansas City. The heart of the business district, with the First National Bank building, is visible in the center of the photograph; on the right edge of the photo is the Kansas City Savings Association Bank at Third and Delaware. Only three blocks to the northwest is Westport Landing, where early steamboats unloaded their cargo before heading up the Missouri River to northern ports. Strong currents and debris just beneath the river's muddy surface made this the most dangerous part of the boats' journey. Two steamships that capsized here were the *Saluda* in 1852, with a loss of up to one hundred people, and the *Arabia*, which sank in 1856.

Thanks to the Gillis family's donation, this site still remains a market area. Its proximity to Westport Landing makes the new display building on the east side of the square an ideal setting for the Treasures of the Steamboat Arabia. In November of 1991, this museum opened to display artifacts recovered by Bob Hawley, his sons Bob and Dave, and their friend Jerry Mackey. They discovered the *Arabia* lying in silt and water under a cornfield near Parkville, Missouri. After devising painstaking ways of digging and pumping the water, they were finally able to retrieve artifacts that were preserved by the sandy silt in near-perfect condition. The recovery team developed many methods for restoring the items, all of which would have been found in a typically stocked general store in 1856.

Designed by architect Asa Beebe Cross, the Pacific House hotel was built at Fourth and Delaware in 1860. In a scrapbook belonging to the Elizabeth Benton Chapter of the Daughters of the American Revolution, the hotel was referred to as "Palatial Pacific House." Civil War documents show that in 1863, the Pacific House quartered General Thomas Ewing and served as a Union Army headquarters. Order #11 was issued here by General Ewing, requesting that all civilians leave the counties of Jackson and Bates, and parts of Vernon County. The intent was to discourage Missouri residents from aiding border guerrillas, and thus helping the Confederate army. Many people refused to leave because they feared losing both their land and possessions. After much suffering as people left homes and crops, Ewing issued Order #20, which offered limited resettlement to "loyal persons." The Pacific House hotel, shown here in 1869, reverted to private use after the war and hosted visits by presidents Abraham Lincoln and Ulysses S. Grant.

In recent years, the Pacific House has had a variety of uses. In 1950, J. M. Baptiste's company, United Chemical, moved into the building. By the 1980s, the hotel was experiencing hard times. The surrounding area, then known as River Quay, became run-down; it attracted seedy businesses and was often disrupted by mobsters who resorted to gunfire and bombings. In the 1990s the area was cleaned up and its name reverted to River Market. The Pacific House was converted into loft apartments in 1999. Today, a charming courtyard across the street lends the building a calm ambience not often found in urban areas.

When Kansas City was little more than a village, it was competing with other towns along the river for the railroad bridge. Efficient delivery was essential for continued growth and development of the West. Kansas City leaders Kersey Coates and Robert Van Horn convinced Congress and the Hannibal Railroad to build the first bridge across the Missouri River in their town. Octave Chanute, a native of Paris, undertook the difficult architectural task. As this photograph from July 3, 1869, shows, opening-day celebrations were elaborate.

Crowds seated along the banks watched *Hannibal* (the prize engine of the Hannibal and St. Joseph Railroad) cross from the north side pulling ten passenger cars, two Pullman cars, and George Pullman's newest invention, the dining car. Pullman watched along with hundreds of citizens who cheered as the engine stopped on the south shore. People scrambled up the hillside for festivities that included a barbeque in the market square. That night, four hundred people attended a sumptuous feast held at the Coates House Hotel.

The original bridge is still visible from an overlook at the river's edge at First and Main, and the broken cement of early streets can also be seen, partly hidden by brush. The first Hannibal Bridge served the railroad until 1917, when a new Hannibal Bridge was completed one hundred feet west of the original. It is still used today by the Burlington Northern and Santa Fe railroads. The white bridge west of the railroad bridge is the Broadway Bridge used by motorists. Nearby, various factories are being converted to loft spaces for residential use. Two blocks southeast is the River Market Square, where the revelers gathered on that memorable day in 1869 to watch the first railroad car cross the Missouri River.

The Barton Brothers Shoe Factory is located at Sixth and Wyandotte. Its cornerstone states that it has been certified on the National Register of Historic Buildings. This 1920s image shows its main entrance, on the west side of the building. Other manufacturing companies in the garment district included Brand and Puritz, M. Reicher and Sons, Fried-Seigel, Alaskan Furs, Backstrom-Fergueson Tailors, Burnham-Munger Shirts, White Goods Manufacturing, Dean Jones Manufacturing, and Quality Hill Dress Company. The Kansas City clothing industry reached its peak in the 1930s and 1940s and at one time employed as many as eight thousand people. Not only did workers prosper, but each company employed salesmen who traveled throughout the country, bringing income to businesses in other regions.

By the late 1960s the once-profitable manufacture of wholesale clothing was no longer possible as consumers continued to demand products at lower prices. The garment district's large multistory buildings, which once housed showrooms, offices, heavy equipment, and storage space, are now being converted into loft apartments and spacious offices. Large windows typically overlook scenes of the river, while high-rises enjoy beautiful views of downtown. The garment district is considered to be the area from Broadway on the east to Locust on the west; the north-south boundary is the River Market to Ninth Street. The building that housed the Barton Brothers Shoe Company in the 1920s has been modernized inside and out. Converted into loft apartments, it is now called SoHo East. This image shows the east side of the building.

This parade with horse-drawn, flower-draped wagons was photographed in 1890. The view is looking north along Main Street, from the southeast corner of Seventh Street. This parade is probably one of Kansas City's famous "Priests of the Pallas" harvest festival celebrations. The celebrations—held from 1887 until 1924—were styled after the Mardi Gras parades in New Orleans. Later, floats were built on streetcar flats and routed through the city on the streetcar rails. Dignitaries lined the balconies of fashionable hotels to view the ornate floats. Other celebrations of Priests of the Pallas were social events where invited guests received collectible memorabilia. The buildings in the background have elegantly decorated windows advertising men's clothing. Buyers would visit the first-floor showrooms to place their orders and their garments would be made in the same building on the floors above.

Following the parade's route through downtown Kansas City today would lead one to the entrance ramps of Interstates 35 and 70. This image vividly shows how the 1960s interstate system literally cut the garment district of Kansas City in two. The northern area, now called River Market, struggled at first but the large brick buildings that stood vacant after a manufacturing decline in the 1960s are being renovated and sold as loft spaces. Developers saw the structurally sound buildings as a great opportunity to improve the River Market area. Many of the garment district buildings succumbed to the wrecking ball during the highway construction but some still remain on the north and south areas adjacent to the interstates.

The foundation was laid for the Coates House Hotel in the early 1860s but it was initially used for cavalry barns and barracks in support of the Union effort in the Civil War. Kersey Coates, a Pennsylvania lawyer and entrepreneur, owned the first bank in Kansas City and opened the landmark Kansas City store Emery, Bird, Thayer. Coates was instrumental in the development of railroads and made a trip to Washington to ensure Congress passed the bill that gave Kansas City the first bridge over the Missouri River. Coates's hotel, shown here in 1900, was positioned at the southeast corner of Tenth and Broadway. Located on the main route of most parades, the hotel offered prime views of many Kansas City celebrations.

The Coates House Hotel is now part of a marketing campaign for one- and two-bedroom apartments and executive suites. A portion of the first floor is currently leased to a hair salon. The neighborhood surrounding the hotel is undergoing change as more lofts are constructed in the garment district. Two blocks west of Broadway, the Pennsylvania Street corridor from Eighth to Fourteenth has already had many restorations. It is hard to believe that in 1860 this land was all part of Kersey Coates's farm, with cattle grazing nearby. Many people in Kansas City remember the Coates House Hotel fire on January 28, 1976, which killed twenty people. Newspaper archives contain haunting stories and photographs of that fateful night. The section of the hotel that was destroyed by fire was never rebuilt.

Coates Opera House was opened in 1871 at the northwest corner of Tenth and Broadway, across the street from the Coates House Hotel. The cost of the theater was $185,000. Opening night featured an opera based on Edward Bulwar-Lytton's play, *Money*. The image above shows the opera house in 1900, in the theater's heyday. Kersey Coates owned the theater but it was his wife Sarah, a highly educated Quaker from Pennsylvania, who was interested in adding culture to this frontier "Town of Kansas" by promoting opera.

After the Civil War ended, she became a cultural and civic force to be reckoned with. For more than thirty years, the Coates Opera House offered Italian and French operas to capacity audiences of 1,800 people. The opera house thrived because visitors could stay at the hotel, stable their horses nearby, and enjoy the opera during their stay. As the building burned to the ground on January 31, 1901, the evening's performance of *The Barber of Seville* was destined to be the final one.

The Coates Opera House building at 930 Broadway was reconstructed in 1912 in a more modern and less-adorned architectural style. It was built for the Rotenberg and Schloss Company, which sold cigars and other gift items. Today's ground floor tenants are the Family Environmental Company, Envision Group LLC, and the Jinsel Center for Integrated Health. The upper floors are leasing under the apt name of Opera House Lofts, managed by SoHo West. It is interesting to note that the Missouri Federation of Women's Clubs, which Sarah Coates promoted in the 1800s, is still an active civic club today.

When the Municipal Airport was dedicated in 1927, world-famous pilot Charles Lindbergh was a participant. Opened in 1929, it was originally referred to as a "passenger station." Its location at the north end of the Broadway Bridge gave travelers who had business downtown a short drive to make flight connections. As airline use increased, additional facilities for storage and maintenance were built. Many passengers' hearts have skipped a beat as their plane landed—the runways are surrounded by the Missouri River on the south and west, which can give the impression that the plane is about to touch down on water. The view of the skyline in this 1940s picture shows the city's tallest buildings in the center: the thirty-five-story National Fidelity Life Insurance Building, City Hall, the Jackson County Courthouse, and the Power & Light Building.

The airport is now named the Charles B. Wheeler Downtown Airport, after the city's former mayor and current state legislator of Missouri. With the expanded public use of airlines, this airport is primarily used for commercial transport and small private planes. The old passenger terminal is now used for trade shows. In 1972, Kansas City International Airport was built seventeen miles north of downtown; it has three large terminals that serve a variety of airlines. Today's view shows the building boom, as many tall buildings have been added to the skyline. Kansas City's tallest skyscraper is the forty-two-story One Kansas City Place at Twelfth and Main, at the right side of the photograph. The thirty-eight-story Town Pavilion is the second-tallest. Other buildings of interest are the curved lines of the Federal Courthouse and the light green H&R Block National Headquarters. The Wheeler Airport began a $270-million renovation in 2006.

This 1926 photograph looks west from the Lewis and Clark Overlook. The Twelfth Street Viaduct is in the upper left-hand corner of the photo; the Eighth Street Bridge is in the foreground. The Eighth Street Bridge went east, tunneling through the steep hillside to join the streetcar system that connected downtown Kansas City with the West Bottoms. Early Kansas City benefited from both bridges, especially workers from the West Bottoms who had to climb many steep steps in all kinds of weather until the Eighth Street

Bridge began to serve the area. The Twelfth Street Viaduct, which was completed in 1900, was important because it was used to transport goods in and out of the industrial area. Although railcars did much of the shipping, local goods needed a roadway to navigate this steep incline. At the lower edge of the photo you can see Kersey Coates Drive. The two-lane road with a lighted and landscaped median was the curving route to picturesque Hyde Park Homes.

The Twelfth Street Viaduct is as useful today as it was in 1900. The Eighth Street Bridge was torn down when the increased use of cars made this small section of railway obsolete. Reinforcements to the Twelfth Street Viaduct have allowed it to carry heavy equipment and goods, thus keeping the West Bottoms a viable area for manufacturing. It has also provided easy access from downtown to the West Bottoms without a long southern route. Gone is the picturesque little road called Kersey Coates Drive; in its place is Interstate 35. The limestone terrace still exists below West Terrace Park, joining in the long park property from Eighth almost to Eleventh Street, overlooking the West Bottoms. Gone also are the stockyards, but behind the Twelfth Street Viaduct the white arches of the American Royal Building, the Kemper Arena, and the red bricks of the Stock Exchange Building are still visible.

Kersey Coates's farm and residence was built at Tenth and Pennsylvania, just two blocks from his hotel and opera house. He had purchased the 110 acres for a group of Pennsylvania investors but they were dissatisfied with the investment and demanded he "get rid of that riverfront property." Kersey decided to buy the land himself and in 1859 he built a home on the farm overlooking the West Bottoms, where he and his wife, Sarah, raised their four children. On the residence, seen here circa 1860, livestock roamed the area north to the Eighth Street overlook and around both the hotel and opera house. Kersey and Sarah were raised as Quakers and avowed pacifists but during the Civil War, when times were so dangerous, they both slept with loaded pistols at their bedside. Sarah became a civic force in the community after the Civil War. She encouraged members of the Philadelphia Emigrant Aid Society to settle here, supported the Women's Suffrage Club, and became a personal friend of the women's civil rights leader Susan B. Anthony.

After his death in 1887, Coates's farm was divided and a portion was named West Terrace Park. This park overlooked what was Kersey Coates Drive at the base of the high limestone terrace. The road curved to the east and wound through the Hyde Park Homes area, with its beautiful houses and hills. Today, a visitor to the site will see a parking lot where the mansion once stood and a community garden to benefit food pantries cultivated by the DST Company. The residence of David Slater (obscured by trees in this photograph) was built after Kersey Coates's death and is now on the National Register of Historic Places. Renovated by Robert Reuben in 1988, it is still inhabited. From West Terrace Park, you can enjoy views of the Twelfth Street Viaduct, the West Bottoms, and the Lewis and Clark Viaduct all the way to downtown Kansas City across the river to the city of Kansas City, Missouri. Just below, the traffic of Interstate 35 follows the path of what was originally Kersey Coates Drive.

This Queen Anne–style mansion at 1032 Pennsylvania was built in 1888 for Elizabeth Allman after the death of her husband, Major Gerald N. Blossom. The land was part of the estate of Kersey Coates. Major Blossom operated the Blossom House Hotel on Union Avenue near the Union Depot in the West Bottoms. It was a very popular hotel with railroad travelers and the livestock traders and ranchers who came to Kansas City to do business. In

1902, William Volker, a Kansas City philanthropist, purchased 1032 Pennsylvania and converted the house into a hotel called the Girl's Association. An additional building (at right in this 1930s photograph) was built in 1928 for the Girl's Club, a boardinghouse for working women. The architectural style and varied coloring of the bricks were dramatic changes from the earlier mansion.

In 1947 Volker's estate sold the mansion and adjoining building to the Catholic Diocese of Kansas City, which operated the complex as the Penn Lodge for Women. Arnold Garfinkel purchased the property in 1971 and present owners Barnett and Shirley Helzberg bought the mansion and additional buildings from the Garfinkel estate. Today, the contrast of the buildings—now connected by an airy glass walkway—seems a charming combination. The property includes two additional buildings and is adjacent to West Terrace Park, with a sweeping view of the valley to the west and north.

This is Kansas City's first stockyard building, built in 1880. A second livestock exchange was opened in 1895 just before the stockyards began a major expansion; the image above is from 1880. Ever since the Hannibal Railroad Bridge was built across the Missouri River in 1869, cattle began arriving from other states and packing plants such as Armour and Swift & Company opened to process the animals. The railcars then transported the meat to more-populated areas east of Kansas City. Transactions at the stockyard trade were oral and sealed with a handshake. The flooding in the West Bottoms often created problems for the livestock industry and the railroads, as well as for laborers who lived and worked in the area. Flooding demanded emergency measures to save livestock. In a 1903 flood, livestock were guided to safety through gates leading to the upper floors of the building. Damage to the foundation was extensive, so a third building was built in 1910 at 1600 Genessee.

The photo today shows the American Stockyard Exchange Building that was built after the floods in 1910. It housed the Stockyard Bank and offered office space to many traders and buyers for the packing plants in the West Bottoms, until stockyard trade ended in 1990. The demise of the stockyard came about by modern refrigerated trucking, which made processing the animals in areas of production less expensive. A highway in the stockyards area has been named for the president of the Kansas City Stockyards Company, Jay B. Dillingham. The livestock industry brought many other types of auxiliary businesses and these companies now have offices in the Kansas City Live Stock Exchange building. Gone now are all the stockyard pens that once held hogs, cattle, and sheep.

The American Royal first started as the "Fat Stock Shows." Early businessmen such as August Meyer and William R. Nelson had country estates in the surrounding areas and they liked to show off their cattle herds, often imported from Europe. Horses were added after they became more of a hobby than a necessity in the mid-1920s. The name was changed to English Royal in 1901 and was later called American Royal. Buildings were erected instead of the tents used in early years. The first building, pictured here in 1950, was built in 1922. Only the hoof-and-mouth quarantine in 1914 and the war years of 1942–45 have ever canceled the American Royal festivities. Each year, parades mark the beginning of the American Royal with rodeo, music shows, schoolchildren touring the animal pens, and the horse shows that have retained the public's interest.

The second building to house the American Royal was built in 1992. The newly remodeled arched and curved entry with a barbecuing cow statue lends a new look and a clue to some of the activities now scheduled within. Permanent offices of the American Royal staff are housed near the spacious entrance. In the fall, a huge barbecuing contest is held with entrants from all over the country, while in the spring, several garden and tractor shows are hosted here. Horse shows and judging of the livestock during the annual Royal festivities take place in the American Royal Arena and show animals are housed and displayed in stalls during the show. The Belles of the American Royal are chosen each fall from young women of college age whose families have contributed to the community.

Until the tractors replaced horses and mules for field work, farmers were always in the market for "good horse flesh." The horse and mule trade was done with traders, including Sparks Brothers. The mules in this 1900 photo are being shown to prospective buyers before the auction so that close inspection could be made of their general condition. Auctions began with one or a group of animals being led into the ring. Statistics about the animals were announced and the auctioneer would begin his chant. Buyers were seated in bleachers for bidding—their style of bidding could vary from just a light tip to the hat or a raise of one finger to the pulling of the ear. Three thousand mules were shipped from Kansas City to the mountains of northern Italy for use as pack animals during the early years of World War II. Not to be confused with donkeys, mules are tall and powerful animals—as can be seen by comparing the stature of the mules and the men in this photograph.

A few horse and mule barns remain near Twelfth and Bell, just east of the Stockyards Exchange Building. Most have not been in use since the horse trade dwindled in the late 1950s but stalls and feed bunks, which have been worn smooth by the animals rubbing against the wood, are still in place. Mules can sometimes be seen in the countryside and are used for pulling and other small farm tasks. They can be identified by their ears, which point forward, and their unusually large teeth, which show when they make their hee-haw sound, unlike a horse's neigh. This Spark Brothers building is now owned by Jim Monahan and is currently occupied by the Environmental Science Laboratory.

Grace Church built its vestry in 1870 at 415 West Thirteenth Street. Trinity Church united with the Grace congregation in 1917 and since that time their church has been called the Grace and Holy Trinity Cathedral. The foundation for the cathedral, pictured here in 1920, was laid in 1889. It was designed by Frederick E. Hill, based on the ideas of Cameron Mann, a former rector. By 1935, it was designated a parish and diocesan cathedral. A beautiful Tiffany window was given to the cathedral by Irwin Russell

Kirkwood in memory of William Rockhill Nelson, Ida Houston Nelson, and Laura Nelson Kirkwood. The Hart window, as it is known, was based on Psalm 42, verse 1: "Like as the Hart desireth the water brooks, so longeth my soul after thee, O God." In 1929 a fire in the chancel area necessitated breaking the Tiffany window—see inset opposite—to vent the fire. Fortunately, the exact blueprints were on file at Tiffany Studios and the window was duplicated in 1930.

Changes to the cathedral have been made through the years. Haden Hall was added in 1954 as an education center. A Gabriel Kney organ was installed in 1982 and renovated in 2004. The exterior of the cathedral was restored in 1987 after the north stone wall collapsed. Stained glass windows in addition to the 1930 Hart window promote serenity and provide a beautiful setting for worship. In 1985, an addition was made to the east side of the church property and was designed by architect Steven Abend.

This building is dedicated for use as a fellowship hall and community soup kitchen. Thousands of meals are served every month to the poor and homeless. Resurgence of residency downtown has allowed children's programs to flourish. The cathedral's outreach program also sponsors a rent and utilities assistance program. Participation in Eucharist is at noon, and there are multiple worship services every weekend.

In 1834, father Benedict Roux purchased forty acres of land at Eleventh and Broadway with funds from the Society for Propagation of Faith in Lyons, France. The log church, seen here in 1860, was often called "Chouteau's Church" because Francois Chouteau, who owned the American Fur Trade Company, provided most of the funds to build it. Father Bernard Donnelly began serving the log church in 1845 and was the priest for thirty-four years. He began making bricks in a kiln at the church and sold them, using the profits to finance many Catholic institutions. The bluff to the west of the church property yielded limestone that was used to shore up the muddy banks along the Missouri River to prevent erosion and give cleaner access to the riverboat loading areas. In 1856, Donnelly used his own bricks to build a church that served the parish until 1883, when the present cathedral began construction as part of the newly formed Diocese of Kansas City. By 1912, carillon bells were added to a cathedral tower and stained glass windows were installed.

The Cathedral of the Immaculate Conception is a landmark that is visible from many vantage points in Kansas City because of its distinctive steeple. Its dome and steeple are made of gold-leaf and have needlelike spikes that discourage pigeons from roosting. The gold-leaf surface was applied to protect the roof and steeple from weather damage. The current sanctuary was recently redesigned by architects Shaughnessy, Fickel and Scott and remodeled by H. L. Huber Construction to fit the directives of the Vatican. The organ, installed in 2003, is a fifty-rank instrument that was built in Italy by Piero and Francesco Ruffati. The sanctuary in-the-round and central altar encourage interaction between worshippers in the parish and the priests during mass. Kansas City's parishioners are involved in outreach support groups that nurture persons in transition, alleviate hunger with lunches, and give emergency assistance and legal and care services.

Municipal Auditorium was built in the early 1930s on the site of the old convention hall. It was financed by a capital improvements special election with overwhelming voter approval, and was dedicated in 1936. The auditorium project, pictured here in 1940, provided over two thousand jobs for unemployed men during the depression. A grant from the Public Works Administration provided about 25 percent of the funding. Historians report that contractor Tom Pendergasts's strong leadership of the Democratic Party in Kansas City and Missouri helped Franklin D. Roosevelt win the presidency, and the grant was given as a reward of political support. Even this theory does not diminish Kansas City's grand Art Deco auditorium, built using limestone, concrete, and steel. The two architectural firms that designed the building were Gentry, Voscamp & Neville and Hoit, Price & Barnes. The Golden Gloves Association of America and various car and boat shows rented the facilities, which included the Arena, Music Hall, and Little Theater.

For seventy years, the Municipal Auditorium has offered Kansas City varied entertainment, from Elvis Presley to the Barnum and Bailey Circus to the symphony orchestra. The auditorium at Twelfth and Wyandotte is within easy access of metropolitan-area residents. With the $14-million makeover contract awarded in May 2006 to the Konrath Group and to be constructed by the Malco Construction Company, touring Broadway shows will now have space to perform on the Music Hall stage. Funds for Music Hall renovations come from a $129-million municipal bond sale that will also improve Bartle Exposition Hall, Kemper Arena, and the Municipal Auditorium garage. The controversial sculptures on top of Bartle Hall (not shown here) were intended to carry out the Art Deco design, but they seem to evoke a more contemporary theme: when they were installed in 1994, R. M. Fischer called his design *Sky Stations*, but many observers call them "Hair Curlers."

The extravagance of the roaring twenties is readily apparent in the Art Deco style of the President Hotel. Built in 1926 and shown here in 1950, the hotel was managed by Frank Dean, president of the Dean Hotel Company, who had managed the Baltimore Hotel since the death of his father, Delevon Dean. Many services and amenities were available—even a lobby pharmacy, operated by Jacob Silverforb. The headquarters for the 1928 Republican National Convention that nominated Herbert Hoover were located here. Charles Lindbergh attended the banquet that the hotel hosted for the dedication of the Municipal Airport. Dining areas included the Round-Up Cocktail Bar and the Drum Room, and there were two ballrooms, the Aztec Room and the grand Congress Room. Many Kansas Citians have memories of seeing Frank Sinatra, Benny Goodman, Tommy Dorsey, and Sammy Davis at the President.

After being closed for twenty-five years, the Hilton President Kansas City opened in January of 2006 with Peter Werner as general manager. The historic hotel was restored—with the help of a $46 million budget—to its original glory. At the same time, the hotel was updated to meet the needs and demands of current hotel patrons. Its 453 small rooms were redesigned to 213 large rooms. The spacious lobby with ornate columns reflects the colors and styles associated with the President's original 1920s design. The Congress Ballroom still boasts magnificent views over Kansas City while the Walnut Dining Room and Drum Room offer sophisticated venues to wine and dine. The famous red drum over the corner entrance is where patrons gain access to the bar and restaurant. The legendary white sign atop the hotel once again tells all that the President is back to stay.

When Thomas W. Lamb and the Boiler brothers of Kansas City designed the 3,500-seat Loew's Midland Theater in 1927, the cost was over $4 million. This photograph was taken in May 1927, before construction was completed. The outstanding exterior feature of the building is the arched Greek column designs on the south wall. On opening night, ornate art objects, thick Oriental carpets, and five massive Czechoslovakian hand-cut glass chandeliers decorated the lobby. The theater used the first six floors of the building with an entrance on Thirteenth and Main. The twelve-story Midland Office Building entrance faced Baltimore Street. It was unique that a single building should be built for multipurpose use in the 1920s.

In 1961 the theater was turned into a bowling alley but in 1966, American Multi-Cinema purchased the theater and renamed it the Midland Theater. During the 1960s the movie theater showed classics on a large screen including *The Sound of Music*, *Fiddler on the Roof*, and *Funny Girl*. By 1977, it was listed on the National Register of Historic Places and was used only for live stage shows, concerts, or performing art groups. Current plans are for the Cordish Company to develop the Midland Theater as a live music club and restaurant. Plans for a $60-million renovation include both the Midland and Empire theaters. The Empire Theater would be a six-screen movie house with a restaurant. Convenient parking for these theaters will be available when J. E. Dunn completes three new parking garages in the H&R Block, Inc., development.

The horses and buggies in this circa 1900 photo of the New York Life Insurance Company emphasize how difficult an engineering feat the building's construction was in 1890. The Renaissance Revival–style building with ten-story wings is joined in the center by a 170-foot tower. Stones for the foundation were from a local quarry. It took four mules to haul each block to the building site. The bricks used on the exterior of the upper floors were made by the McClelland, Stumpf and Pelzer Brick Company, which operated a kiln at Third and Wyandotte. The first three floors' exteriors used brownstone that was shipped from Vermont for a contrast in color and texture. When the New York Life building was completed, it became Kansas City's tallest structure. Important features of the building that have contributed to its long use are the fireproof construction and the use of natural light with windows on all sides.

The New York Life Insurance Company has one of downtown Kansas City's most famous outdoor sculptures and it has guarded the entrance of 20 West Ninth since 1891. The sculptor, Louis Saint-Gaudens, was one of the leading American artists to adopt realism when he designed the eagle with outspread wings grasping a ball supported at the base by two figures. The building is visible to northbound traffic on Baltimore Avenue, which offers a perfect vantage point of this beautiful building. The architectural firm of Gastinger, Walker, Harden received a design award from the AIA in 1996, following rehabilitation by the contractors J. E. Dunn. The current occupants, Aquila, Inc., have developed technology to reduce energy costs with the use of a "chiller," which makes ice at night and cools the building during the day. The interior has advanced systems of telecommunications and adheres to strict use of recycled materials.

The Savoy Hotel sign has been replaced in this 1950 photo and shows only signage for the Savoy Grill. The neoclassical Savoy Hotel and Grill at 219 West Ninth was built in four separate phases. The first phase (1888) was designed by architects Chamberlain, Van Brunt and Howe and constructed of wood framing and steel. The builder was Arbuckle Brothers, which owned the Arbuckle Coffee Company. In 1910, when the Union Depot in the West Bottoms closed and moved to Union Station, the Savoy Hotel became popular with travelers because of its luxurious rooms. When the Savoy Grill opened in 1903, it banned service to women. That restriction was soon lifted and music and dancing filled the room after dinner. The Savoy murals were the work of Edward Holslag. He painted scenes of pioneers departing Westport Landing and depicted their journey before arriving at the end of the Santa Fe Trail.

After the depression, hard times persisted for the Savoy Hotel. However, the Savoy Grill endured, even in the 1960s, when the hotel was in serious financial trouble. By the 1970s it had become a residential hotel for transients just to pay its expenses. The grill has always been popular for its seafood menu and great steaks, beautifully stained wood booths and walls, and its long, carved oak bar. A plaque identifies booth #4 as the President's Booth, where Harry Truman was always served. The Holslag murals have been cleaned and

are still in place, with one now slightly hidden by heating ducts. They are included in the Smithsonian Institution's Bicentennial Inventory of American Paintings. The current owner is Don Lee, who purchased the hotel in 1965 to keep his lease on the restaurant. It was not until 1985 that Lee could begin to renovate a few rooms at a time, turning the old hotel rooms into bed-and-breakfast suites.

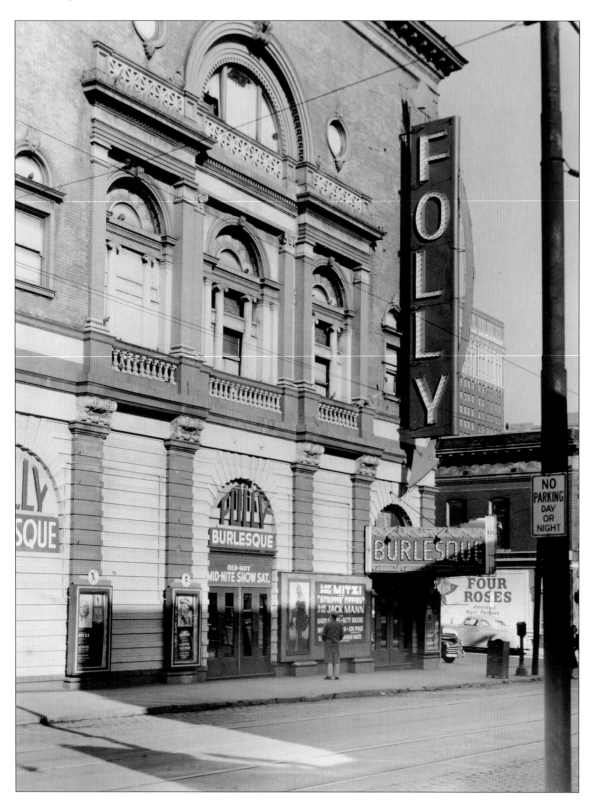

The row of saloons west of Twelfth Street and Wyandotte was a rowdy place in the 1930s. The Folly Theater, on the corner of Twelfth and Central, opened in 1900. Originally known as the Standard Theatre, it was used as a venue for the burlesque shows of James Butler. His father, Colonel Edward Butler, had built the theater, which was designed by Kansas City architect Louis Curtiss. The Shubert family brought in famous acts like the Marx Brothers when they leased the theater in the 1920s. The Great Depression forced closure or reduced budgets in most theaters, but venues like the Folly, pictured here in 1945, were given a new lease on life when World War II attracted soldiers to their burlesque shows.

The years after World War II saw Twelfth Street reduced to liquor stores and cheap bars. It was not until November of 1981 that the Folly reopened as part of Twelfth Street's urban renewal. Its beautifully restored exterior with arched windows, and its spacious lobby and refurbished seating and stage areas, provide an intimate venue for small concerts and recitals. It is now used for regular concerts by the Kansas City Symphony Chorus, the Folly Jazz Series, and barbershop quartets, among others. Convenient parking makes this a pleasant downtown destination.

In 1880 the First Baptist Church built a wood-frame building at Twelfth and Baltimore with a gift of $30,000 from Colonel and Mrs. W. H. Harris. The congregation gathered there for services until 1908, when they built a new sanctuary at Linwood and Park. It wasn't until 1913 that descendants and heirs of George Muehlebach invested $2 million for a new hotel designed by Samuel Whitmore on the church site at Twelfth and Baltimore. Muehlebach was a Swiss immigrant who had come to Kansas City in 1865 from Virginia and who operated a saddle shop and vineyard in Westport. Although not yet part of the landscape in this 1940 photograph, in 1952 the seventeen-story Muehlebach Tower was added and the second Orpheum Theater south of the hotel was demolished to build the Muehlebach Convention Center. This addition provided exhibition and meeting room space on the upper floors. The ground floor tenant was Trans World Airlines.

In its early years, the Muehlebach set the standard for hotel excellence in Kansas City. Harry Truman used the Muehlebach as the Presidential Command Center when he was in Independence during his presidency. Every president from Truman to Gerald Ford visited the hotel. Kansas City businessman Barney L. Allis bought and became manager of the Muehlebach Hotel in 1931. He lived at the hotel until his death in 1962. The Barney Allis Plaza, a parklike patio on top of the Allis Parking Garage adjacent to the hotel, is named in his honor. After the Marriott Corporation assumed ownership of the hotel in 1996, the Muehlebach Tower was demolished and the original registration desk with its pigeonhole mailboxes at the Wyandotte entry was restored. Other interior designs meet historic preservation guidelines. The companies that redesigned the hotel were Westlake Construction and the architectural firm Holabird & Roche. The updated hotel joins the Marriott complex, which includes the Downtown Kansas City Marriott at Twelfth and Wyandotte.

Herndon Estates owned the northeast corner of Twelfth and Baltimore, which had been occupied by a five-story apartment building since 1895. When the property was sold to the Oppenstein brothers in 1919, it was renamed the Glennon Hotel. After the experienced hotelier Charles E. Phillips purchased the Glennon Hotel in 1929, he demolished the building and hired Boilet and Hauk as architects to design the Phillips House Hotel. By 1931 Phillips had built Kansas City's tallest hotel, with 450 rooms on twenty floors, for $1.6 million. Interior features of the Phillips Hotel that charmed the public were its golden *Dawn* statue, depicted as a winged goddess by noted sculptor Jorgen Dreyer, and the entry's "invisible ceiling," created with black mirrors and walnut woodwork. This decor was meant to give a European elegance. As this 1935 photograph shows, the hotel's southeast corner was leased to retail shops, a move typical of European hotels at the time. The Walnut Room was the main dining room and patrons might still recall the Tropics, a third-floor lounge that featured a mechanical dancing hula girl.

After 1971, the Phillips Hotel changed hands many times. The Phillips family closed the hotel and reopened it in 1974 after spending $1.8 million on twenty-two rooms and remodeling the mezzanine and the Cabana Room. One year later the family signed a management agreement with Ramada Inn, Inc. In 1976 the Oppenstein Brothers Charitable Foundation gave the hotel title to Rockhurst University, which was to use only the conference centers in the hotel. Yet another change came about in 1977 when Rockhurst sold the hotel to an Arkansas–New Mexico firm. In 1978 the Phillips Hotel closed and all of its furnishings were sold. When the hotel was placed on the National Register of Historic Places in 1979, it was sold to Phillips House, Ltd., and the firm spent $9 million on renovations. From 1990 to 1998, Radisson Hotels operated the Phillips Hotel. Marcus Hotels, the current owners, restored the hotel to its former glory with a grand opening in 2001.

The First National Bank at the northeast corner of Tenth and Baltimore was just one of the many buildings built in what was referred to as "Banker's Row." There were no formal zoning laws mandating that businesses be clustered by trade, but the garment industry was grouped near the Market Square area by the river, the hotels were along Twelfth Street, and the banks were along Tenth. The First National Bank building, seen here circa 1903, was constructed in four phases. In the first phase of 1904, the original three-story bank building had large Ionic columns and heavy bronze doors at its main entrance. In 1926, the original architects designed a fourth floor and a four-story annex to the north side. Founded by Iowa native Edward Holden in 1866, the bank's early business was to finance the livestock trade. The bank's first president was Taylor Abernathy, whose family owned the Abernathy Furniture Company. Edward Swinney, who came to Kansas City in 1857, started as a cashier and eventually became the bank's president.

The third renovation of the bank was in 1964, when a marble-sheathed five-story expansion was designed by Marshall and Brown. First National Bank occupied the building until 1971. When Boatman's Bank merged with Mark Twain Bank, they vacated the building. Kansas City then spent two years on major renovations to the building so that it could accommodate the Kansas City Central Public Library. Designed by HNBT and opened in the spring of 2004, it is a beautiful use of space. The lobby features a snack bar and information booth on the first level. Upstairs are the Missouri Valley Resource Room and meeting rooms. A huge mural depicting books on a bookshelf is on the wall of the parking garage adjoining the library. Two other buildings constructed at the same time as First National Bank, Kansas City Life Insurance Company and the Nelson-Atkins Museum of Art, used granite from the same quarry in Indiana.

A cable car is shown heading west down Ninth Street in this photograph from 1890. A southbound cable car on Walnut Street can be seen at the top of the hill. This steep incline was a thrilling ride when the car came to a stop at the bottom of Ninth and Main—especially on hot days, when the cable stretched a little. The intersection at Ninth and Main is where Jacob Keefer, a Pennsylvania financier, built Planter's House, later known as the Atlantic House and then Vaughn's Diamond Building. In the 1930s, the roof was famous for its billboard use. Many old photographs show the billboard advertisement, "Owl Cigars." When the Westgate Hotel was built on the same location in 1915, its room rates ranged from $1.50 to $2.00 a night. A flagpole sitter named Shipwreck Kelly was well known for staying up on the flagpole outside the Westgate Hotel in below-freezing temperatures for up to six days.

Transportation improvements in braking and the low speed limits of downtown Kansas City have reduced the excitement of the old Ninth and Main intersection. The Westgate Hotel in the center island of Ninth and Main was demolished in 1954 and was replaced in 1963 by a sculpture and fountain titled *The Muse of Missouri* (beyond the left of this picture). Sponsors for the fountain were James M. Kemper and the Downtown Redevelopment Company. Architects Simpson & Murphy and Hare & Hare, and sculptor Wheeler Williams received awards for their contributions to the area. The walkway across Ninth Street links the Commerce parking lot on the north side of the street with the Commerce Towers Office Building on the south side.

In 1909, when architect Louis Curtiss designed the Boley Building at Twelfth and Walnut, he experimented with the idea of using a transparent glass wall to enclose the entire structure. Sometimes referred to as the "Hanging Glass Building," the facade included arched windows in a vertical line, interspaced with vertical, straight-line windowpanes. Curtiss, who worked from nearby offices, designed in a wide variety of styles including Prairie, Art Deco, and Craftsman, as well as the Art Nouveau style he chose for the Boley Building, seen here in 1910. Walnut Street was a busy area that attracted many shoppers. Over the years the ground floor was occupied by a variety of retail tenants, including the Katz Drug Store. A tragedy occurred in January 1917 when gas tanks exploded inside the building, spraying glass shards onto the street below, killing two pedestrians and injuring another fifty-two.

By 1978 the Boley Building was no longer the center of a busy downtown retail area and could be found next to lower-rent tenants such as Gigi's Wigs and Beauty Supplies. The Boley Building has recently been used as an art space and in 2006 it housed the Urban Culture Art Center, displaying local artists' work. Next to the Boley Building is the 1201 Walnut building that houses Kansas City Power & Light. The prestigious H&R Block Headquarters development is under construction across the street. The charcoal Art Nouveau exterior of the Boley Building still retains its distinctive look among these newer developments.

The first building on this site in the 1880s was the Federal Government Office, which housed a post office, customs office, and United States Courthouse. In 1902, the federal government sold the building to Fidelity National Bank & Trust Company. In 1929 Fidelity demolished the original building and constructed the present thirty-five-story skyscraper with its twin towers. Designed by the architects Hoit, Price, and Barnes and seen here in the 1930s, the building was considered fireproof because of its steel frame and concrete floors and exterior. In 1946, the federal government purchased the new building to use as office space. The famous clock tower was so accurate that it was used to set watches. However, due to the operational time and costs involved in keeping the clock running, it was only used until the 1950s.

In 1970 the Fidelity National was again being used as a federal office building. The government's weather bureau used the radar tower's weather ball as a storm warning system. In 1972, the clock was taken down for fear that parts would fall onto the street below. In 2006, this landmark Kansas City high-rise was rechristened the 909 Walnut Building. The property is now managed by Simbol Commercial and has thirty stories devoted to residential rental space. The first two floors are leased to Perfect Commerce and there are plans to include a restaurant and inside parking. On the front of the building you can still read the original name in stone, Fidelity National Bank.

Hale's Water Tower in action.

Walnut bet. 8th & 9th

Founding members of the Walnut Street Methodist Church established a congregation in 1844 and later moved to Eleventh and Paseo. The fire station was next door to the church and in this circa 1895 photograph a "Hale's Water Tower" is visible in the center. George Hale was a member of the first paid fire department and was promoted to fire chief in 1889. He developed new ways to improve firefighting and by 1891 he had invented the "Swinging Harness" to hitch horses quickly, as well as the Hale's Water Tower, a hose device attached to a mobile horse-drawn fire engine. At the height of his career in 1902, Mayor James Reed fired Hale for not approving an alarm system that was later proved faulty. Undeterred, Hale unveiled his second fire engine, which used a gas engine, in 1904 at the St. Louis World's Fair.

The Walnut Street Church membership has moved to its current location at Fifty-second and Oak, as part of the Central United Methodist Church. Pastor Adam Hamilton and a small core group from Central Church founded the United Methodist Church of the Resurrection in 1990. Their membership exceeded 15,000 in 2006. The site of the old church and fire station is now occupied by a parking garage. Kansas City firefighters have faithfully served their community since 1878. In 1988, firefighters answered a call for a fire in a trailer that contained explosives. Upon arrival, the fire engine exploded and all six crewmembers were killed, the highest number of deaths in the department's history. There is a Firefighter Fountain, designed by Bryan Gash, at Thirty-first and Broadway, honoring those who have died serving their city. Erected in 1991, it bears the inscription, "They who give their lives for others shall be exalted on High and enshrined in our memory forever."

V. 745

This photograph shows the Kansas City Club draped with bunting and displaying a street banner that announces it as the Democratic National Committee headquarters of the 1900 Democratic National Convention. The club was originally used by gentlemen who lived in the Quality Hill area. Chided by their wives for smoking cigars after dinner, they formed their own club. Their first venue, a rented room at the Coates House Hotel, was followed by a move to a storefront on Eleventh and Broadway. However, after an increase in membership, plans were made for this permanent clubhouse. The five-story building at the northeast corner of Twelfth and Wyandotte was built in 1887. Land was purchased for $42,000 and the construction costs were $70,000. Over the years the club has had many distinguished members and honorary members, including Harry S. Truman and Dwight D. Eisenhower. The club's founding president was the Kansas City banker and lawyer Abia A. Tomlinson.

The Kansas City Club moved to its present home at Thirteenth and Baltimore in 1920. The new venue was elaborate and functional, with a large gymnasium, swimming pool, eating facilities, and six full floors of bedrooms for members and their guests. The old Twelfth and Wyandotte site was prime real estate—close to the financial district, the Municipal Auditorium, and Bartle Hall—when it was purchased in 1985. Opening under the name Allis Plaza, this hotel was sold to the Marriott Corporation in 1987 and the name was changed to the Marriott Downtown. At the same time, Marriott acquired the historic Muehlebach Hotel for renovation. Both hotels are now managed by the Raphael Hotel Group for Marriott Corporation and they are joined by the walkway shown in this photograph. The twenty-two-story complex has over a thousand rooms and suites and includes light display features that change design with the seasons.

V-621-2
7333

No street in Kansas City has ever matched the fame of Eleventh Street from Grand Avenue west to Main Street, which was affectionately called "Petticoat Lane." Some think the origin of the name is derived from London's "rag trade" market of the same name. Others assume it was named after the number of women's retail stores on the street, but the true origin is unknown. At the east end, shoppers enjoyed the Emery, Bird, Thayer store. Midway down Eleventh they stopped off at Woolf Brothers Clothing for elegant menswear, or would cross the street to visit Harzfeld's, a full-service women's shop. Shoppers came to see holiday decorations in the streets and store windows, especially Harzfeld's, which boasted animated windows for every season. John Taylor Dry Goods, seen at the end of the street in this photo from 1920, opened in 1918. Taylor parked his wagons and horses just north of the store. The Bryant building, built in 1931, was at the southwest corner of Eleventh and Grand.

It was not until the late 1960s that shoppers moved on from this once-busy street. As seen here in 2006, it is mostly deserted at midday. The Emery, Bird, Thayer building was demolished in 1973. Its elevator cages are now installed as private dining booths at a restaurant called EBT at the state line and Interstate 435. The mezzanine level where ladies had enjoyed their lunches has now been replaced by the United Missouri Bank corporate headquarters. Built in 1986, the bank was designed by Abend Singleton. The chief officers of UMB trace their banking heritage back to the 1890s and William Kemper, whose son R. Crosby Kemper Sr. was chairman of the board until 1967. R. Crosby Kemper III resigned as board chairman in 2004. Down the block toward Main, the Harzfeld's women's store and the Woolf Brothers shop for men have both closed.

The Paseo was built as part of the "City Beautiful" planning that began in 1880. Named after the Paseo de la Reforma of Mexico City, this intersection at Twelfth and Paseo has a flower- and vine-covered pergola just behind the stone wall (at the far right in this circa 1909 photograph) and a fountain (visible in the photo opposite). The Spanish Cannon, a gift from Theodore Roosevelt for patriotism at the beginning of World War I, guards the Sunken Gardens. The gardens and fountain were dedicated on May 30, 1922, in memory of William Fitzsimmons, MD, a Kansas City native and University of Kansas graduate who was the first American officer killed in World War I. Legionnaires, physicians, and bands paraded for the five thousand spectators at the ceremony. This photo shows the Central Methodist South Church in the distance behind the fountain, and the New York and Circle apartment buildings in the foreground.

The Paseo roadway was relocated in 1974, eliminating the sharp turn at the retaining wall at Twelfth Street, now a one-way eastbound street. The Spanish Cannon was moved fifty feet east and the old Sunken Gardens were leveled and relandscaped by the Park Board of Kansas City. This photo taken in early spring 2006 shows the circular gardens ready for planting.

Scars of fire and age show on the apartment building on the left—its pillars remain but are in need of restoration. The old buildings to the east were razed and replaced by new housing as part of the Twelfth and Vine urban renewal projects.

The two-story Blue Room at Eighteenth and Vine was built in the early 1900s by Ethel Palmer. From 1920 to 1930 the Blue Room, shown here in 1915, played host to two of Kansas City's most famous jazz clubs, the Mayflower and the Toy & Toy. Growth of industry and expansion of the stockyards in the West Bottoms, combined with floods there in 1903 and 1951, caused a population shift in the black community. Relocation took place near Twelfth and Vine. The Eighteenth and Vine neighborhood remains as the only relatively intact physical remnant of Kansas City's jazz heritage. Kansas City had 120 nightclubs and forty dance halls in the 1930s; most featured jazz music and a mix of styles from New Orleans, Memphis, and Arkansas that came to be known as the "Kansas City style." It was made famous by Charlie "Bird" Parker, William "Count" Basie, Bennie Moten, Walter Page, and Oliver Todd.

The area surrounding Eighteenth and Vine had another influx of people in the 1950s, when Interstate 35 was built. The Attucks Urban Renewal Project razed jazz venues in slum areas and Vine Street experienced a downturn of business. However, the population maintained its interest in jazz because of the Mutual Musicians Local #627 Hall at 1812 Highland, a spot for informal jam sessions. The leaders of Kansas City realized how vital it was to preserve the city's jazz culture. They sold city bonds to help finance the opening of the American Jazz Museum and Negro Leagues Baseball Museum at Eighteenth and Vine in 1997. Today the Blue Room's performances are connected with the Jazz Museum, along with the Peachtree Restaurant, Gem Theater, and Charlie Parker Memorial.

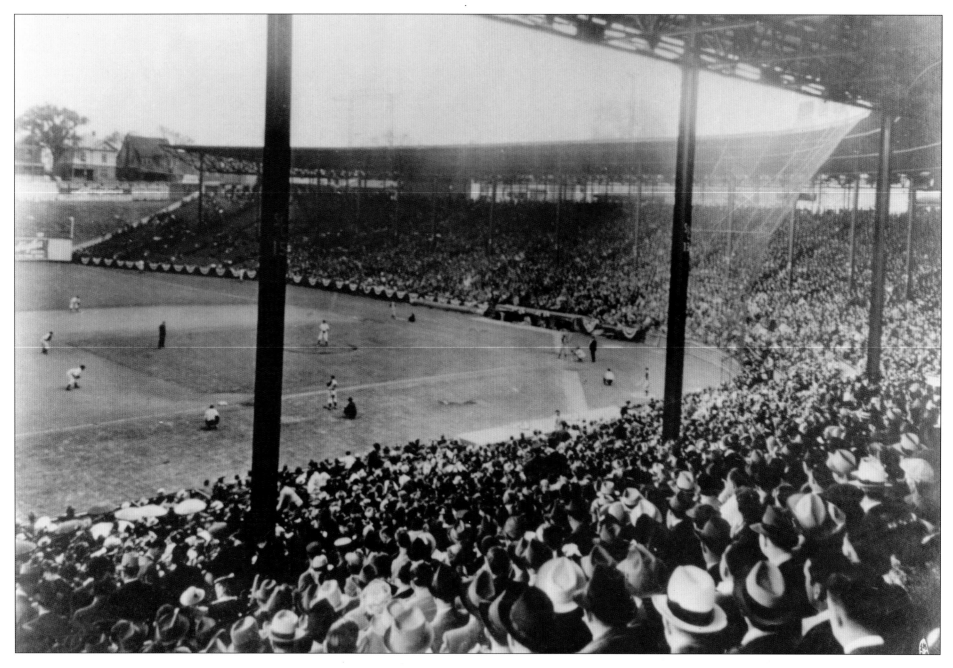

Muehlebach Stadium opened in 1923 with 17,500 seats in two bleachers and a grandstand at Twenty-second and Brooklyn. The stadium's owner, George Muehlebach Jr., owned a brewery, a hotel, and the Blues baseball team. The Blues shared their stadium with the Kansas City Monarchs, who were owned by J. L Wilkinson. By leasing his stadium to both the Blues and Monarchs, Muehlebach had teams playing in his stadium, pictured here in 1950, every night. His stadium and team were sold to the New York Yankees' Jacob Ruppert in 1937 and the stadium was renamed Ruppert Stadium, only to undergo another name change in 1943 when it became the Blues Stadium. Well-known Blues players included Roger Maris and Mickey Mantle; Monarchs player Jackie Robinson broke the major leagues' color barrier in April 1947 when he was signed by the Brooklyn Dodgers.

Chicago businessman Arnold Johnson bought the Philadelphia Athletics in 1954 and moved them to Kansas City. The newly named Municipal Stadium was expanded and renovated to accommodate them. This gave major-league status to Kansas City for the first time. Opening day saw President Harry S. Truman throwing the first pitch in front of 31,895 fans. The A's were sold in 1960 to Charles O. Finley, who later moved the struggling team to Oakland, California, in 1967. In 1969, Kansas City was awarded an expansion team, the Royals, owned by Ewing Kauffman. The Royals were named for Kansas City's American Royal celebration. They were defeated in the 1980 World Series but won in it in 1985. After Kauffman's death in 2000, David Glass became owner of the team. Municipal Stadium was demolished in 1976 and the site is currently being developed for single-family homes. The Truman Complex's Arrowhead and Kauffman stadiums opened in 1973.

This 1920 photograph shows the exclusive St. Regis Hotel, built by Howard Vrooman in 1914. The architectural firm Owens and Payson designed the half-million-dollar structure, which was close to the many apartment buildings that lined Armour Boulevard from the Paseo west to Broadway Street. The interior halls and parlors of the St. Regis were lined with Sienna marble and the exterior was known for its balconies, striped awnings, and porches decorated with colorful flowerpots. When the buildings along this corridor were new, many residents of Kansas City rode public transportation and they flocked to rent in this area, which was conveniently situated on the streetcar lines. Theodore Gary, chairman of the Missouri State Highway Commission, took up permanent residence in a penthouse suite at the St. Regis. At the time, the city's best views were said to be from the hotel's ninth-floor ballroom.

The elegant building at 1400 East Linwood Boulevard is now called the St. Regis Apartments. No longer an exclusive hotel, the building is now owned by Casey Knudson and houses elderly and disabled persons. The lobby has been updated and repainted and rooms have been redesigned for easier access. Although the awnings are gone, the hundred residents can enjoy many of the same features that hotel guests did almost a century ago. The deck on the rooftop still has a remarkable panoramic view of Kansas City.

The distinctive Swope Park entrances were made of native limestone and designed by John Van Brunt and George Kessler in 1902. In this photo from 1909, people are waiting at the entrance for the streetcar that brought people to and from the park. The park opened in 1896 when Colonel Thomas H. Swope gave 1,350 acres of land to the city with the condition that there be no charge for admission. The first shelter house was built just inside the gates and the park's zoo opened in 1909. Kansas City's first public golf course was designed east of the entryway. In 1905, the Evanston Golf Club signed a fifteen-year lease for the Swope residence. Heavily shaded, it had large fireplaces, a dining area with a dance floor, and many bedrooms. Swope died under mysterious circumstances—some believe he was poisoned—on October 3, 1909, at the age of eighty-two.

Today the roads surrounding Swope Park have been paved for cars, but the old stone markers at its entrance remain in place, as does the original shelter house. The Evanston Golf Club and its wooded clubhouse have been replaced by Southeast High School. In 1934, the Swope Memorial Golf Course opened in a quieter area of the park; it is considered to be Kansas City's premier public golf course. Swope Park still contains a zoo, as well as a new IMAX cinema and the open-air Starlight Theater. Outside the gates is a lovely reflecting fountain that is a fitting tribute to the park's benefactor, Colonel Thomas H. Swope.

Edwin W. Shields, owner of Simmonds-Shields-Theis Grain Company, hired architect Thomas Wight to design his estate. Southwood Park, Shields's English country–style home at 5110 Cherry Street, was built in 1913. Wight was a prominent architect who designed the First National Bank of Kansas City and the Kansas City Life Insurance building. The north side of the Shields estate, pictured here in the 1930s, included a carriage house with stables on the lower level and a polo field. The grounds south of the residence featured beautiful gardens and fountains. Wrought-iron fences with brick posts surrounded the property and a curved double wrought-iron gate gave entry to the estate.

The Shields estate was sold to the University of Missouri in 1960. The carriage house was split into two levels, with classrooms on the main floor and meeting rooms in the stable area below. The house is now home to the Henry W. Bloch School of Business and Public Administration. With the financial assistance from the H&R Block Foundation, architect Mel Solomon was able to extend the west end of the building and create a north wing without damaging the building's integrity. It is a beautiful transformation of an elegant home. Inside the new entry, the original stained-glass windows flank the giant oak double doors. The interior still contains the staircase and the long windows that overlook the south lawn as part of the formal entry hall.

The University of Missouri–Kansas City would not have had their present campus without the generosity of businessman and philanthropist William Volker. It was Ernest H. Newcomb who worked diligently writing a charter to get both community and financial support to open the school. He encouraged Volker to buy fifty acres southeast of the Country Club Plaza, which included the residence of Walter S. Dickey (at right in this 1940s image), the millionaire clay pipeline manufacturer. Newcomb was a Southern educator who had been

president of Lincoln and Lee College and served as college business manager between 1933—when classes commenced—and 1938. In its first academic year there were 268 students and a faculty of eighteen. Newcomb Hall (at left) was built in 1936 and originally served as a library. In 1945, President Truman accepted his honorary doctorate from the school and gave a public address from the portico of Dickey Mansion.

William Volker lived to see his university become a thriving school for the metropolitan area. Dickey Mansion was renamed Scofield Hall after the first chancellor of the University of Missouri, Dr. Carleton F. Scofield. The mansion now houses advisory offices for the College of Arts and Sciences and a language resource center. Much of the interior is still intact, including the original ornate fireplace, marble staircase, and walnut paneling. Newcomb Hall now houses offices, the Edgar Snow Collections, and the Western Historical Manuscript Collection. The campus joined the University of Missouri system in 1963 and now includes schools of liberal arts, law, dentistry, and medicine.

This 1950 photo shows the second location of the Menorah Hospital, at 4949 Rockhill Road. The first facility, called the Alfred Benjamin Dispensary, was built by United Jewish Services in 1909 and was located at 1000–1010 Admiral Boulevard. Care was needed for the influx of Jewish immigrants who arrived in Kansas City in the early 1900s and many hospitals at the time only treated patients of their own faith, nationality, or color. In 1931 the Jewish community contributed so generously to this new hospital that they equipped each room with luxuries—including radios and bells for summoning nurses—as well as the standard necessities. The hospital acquired many specialists and prestigious doctors after this expansion.

Menorah Hospital closed its doors in 1995 and moved to Menorah Medical Park at 119th and Nall Avenue in Overland Park, Kansas, where they expanded their patient care to include people of all races and creeds. After Menorah Hospital moved, the building on Rockhill Road was razed. The site was bought by James E. Stowers, founder and chairman of American Century Investments. Stowers, a former medical student, and his wife, a nurse, were both cancer survivors and were keen to donate a facility for medical research. Their $50-million gift led to the construction of a 600,000-square-foot research unit on a ten-acre campus. Alongside its laboratories, the Stowers Institute for Medical Research includes ponds, fountains, and waterways, as well as a thirty-one-foot sculpture of a double helix. Researchers here focus on cancer and other gene-based diseases.

William Rockhill Nelson arrived from Indiana in 1880 to set up the *Evening Star*. He used his newspaper to support causes for reform, particularly city improvements for parks—he was instrumental in hiring George Kessler, the city planner who developed the "City Beautiful" movement. Kessler built a large stone Craftsman-style home at Forty-fifth and Oak as well as one for his daughter, Laura, at Forty-seventh and Rockhill Road. Nelson and his sister, Mary Atkins, a former teacher, wanted their fortunes to go toward building an art museum for the city. Their joint inheritance left $3 million to finance the museum's building and art collection. Architect Thomas Wight designed the museum on the site of Nelson's home in 1932 and it opened the following year. Shown here circa 1935, the museum had no nucleus art collection but was fortunate to find Lawrence Sickman, an expert in Oriental art who procured works during the Great Depression with funds from the Nelson-Atkins trust.

The Nelson-Atkins Museum of Art is the jewel in Kansas City's crown. The beautiful Kirkwood Hall is the spacious entrance to the Greek Renaissance building that can be entered from either north or south. Roselle Court, with its arches, fountain, and stone floors, remains a lovely setting for lunch or parties. The multifloor galleries include a European painting collection with works by artists such as Monet, Degas, Rubens, and Rembrandt. The American painting collection, given by the Enid and Crosby Kemper Foundation, includes works by Eakins, Home, and Church, and the Asian art collection is considered one of the best in the country. Outside visitors can enjoy bronze sculptures by Henry Moore as well Claes Oldenburg and Coosje van Bruggen's larger-than-life *Shuttlecocks* on the front lawn. The first addition to the museum building is presently under construction—the Glass House, estimated to cost $140 million—is due to open in 2007.

August Meyer made his fortune in Kansas City and Leadville, Colorado, from mining and silver. He bought the Kansas City Smelting and Refining Company in 1881. Highly interested in nature, beautiful homes, and landscaping, Meyer served as president of the park board in 1895 and was instrumental in hiring landscaper George Kessler for the city's redevelopment. It was Kessler's designs that made Kansas City renowned for its parks and boulevard systems. Meyer built his home on an 8.5-acre tract at 4415 Warwick Boulevard in 1896. The lavish home, pictured here circa 1900, featured a goldfish lake and landscaping of evergreens. The Flemish Queen Anne–style home had twenty-six rooms and was designed by architects Van Brunt and Howe. Philanthropist Howard Vanderslice purchased the Meyer home in 1928 and donated it to the Kansas City Art Institute.

August Meyer's name has a familiar ring to it in Kansas City. The boulevard extending from Sixty-third and the Paseo to Ward Parkway is called Meyer Boulevard. He is also honored with a bust on the Paseo for his service to the park commission in planning the boulevards and fountains that are still enjoyed today. Vanderslice Hall, as it is now known, has maintained its architectural integrity. Now used as administrative offices for the Kansas City Art Institute, the building was placed on the National Register of Historic Places in 1983.

This photograph, circa 1909, shows Kenwood Golf Links, established in 1894 on Thirty-fourth and Charlotte. The game was difficult here, especially with Westport's "herd law," which did not allow the free-roaming cows to be disturbed. In 1896 the golf club leased a new clubhouse at Fifty-second and Wornall from the Seth Ward estate, where the course remained until 1921. In 1927 Ella Loose bought the land south of Fifty-second and Wornall for $500,000 and turned it into a park in memory of her late husband, Jacob Loose. Jacob, who had come to Kansas City in 1882, founded the Loose-Wiles Biscuit Company—best known for its animal crackers and cartoon cookies. A generous charity worker, Loose initiated the Children's Mercy Hospital Endowment Fund. Mrs. Loose was known as a compassionate and charismatic woman. She was a popular hostess but also a kind benefactor and for more than thirty years she bought shoes for the local orphanage, often rewarding each child with $1 to spend on "foolishness."

In 1946 the company's named changed from Loose-Wiles Biscuits to Sunshine Biscuits; it is now a subsidiary of Keebler. Mrs. Loose was a widow for twenty-two years and spent ten winters as a permanent resident at the Mayflower Hotel in Washington, D.C. Rumor has it that she left the hotel when a cracker of another brand was served at one of her dinner parties. She wanted Loose Park be a "restful place, especially for children," and today it lives up to her wishes, with large open greenways, a wading pool for children, and a beautiful rose garden. The south side of Loose Park has historical markers and a cannon honoring the Battle of Westport. Before her death in 1945, many people experienced Mrs. Loose approaching them and asking, "Are you enjoying my park?" She would then hop back into her chauffered car and return to the Walnuts, a luxury apartment block, where she could survey the park from her penthouse suite.

The house at 1032 West Fifty-fifth was built in 1858 by the Indian trader William Bent and his Cheyenne Indian wife. Bent sold the property in 1871 to fellow Indian trader Seth Ward, who commissioned the architect Asa Beebe Cross to design a two-story addition to the side of the original house, shown here circa 1920. Ward's property included land from the state line to Wornall Road and from Fifty-first to Fifty-fifth. Ward was a Virginian who became a trader and sutler in Fort Laramie, Wyoming, where he bought and sold surplus goods from settlers on the California and Oregon trails. His 1860 marriage to a Westport woman eventually brought him to Kansas City in 1871. He was a Southern Democrat who said he would not shave until the Confederacy won its freedom. He died with the full white beard he had been wearing for forty-one years.

This two-story redbrick antebellum mansion has fourteen rooms, eight fireplaces, and nine porches. The Kansas City Country Club used the Ward farm for a golf course until it moved to Kansas; the house is now privately owned. The Ward land includes the present-day Sunset Hill neighborhood in the country club district. Ward's son, Hugh, married Vassie James Ward Hill, who is considered to be the founder of the Pembroke Country Day School for Boys and the Sunset Hill School for Girls. She headed the Ward Investment Company after Hugh died in 1909 and developed the Sunset Hill area. J. C. Nichols named Ward Parkway in memory of Hugh Ward, who had helped him design a gateway south of the Plaza.